This book is given with love

TO:

_____

FROM:

_____

ISBN: 978-1-949474-44-2

Edition: June 2019

For all inquiries, please contact us at:

info@puppysmiles.org

To see more of our books, visit us at:

www.PuppyDogsAndIceCream.com

THE TEN COMMANDMENTS
LIVING A LIFE OF VIRTUE

WRITTEN BY
Jimmy Lynn

ILLUSTRATED BY
Deborah Valentino

Put God first in your life,
He loves you more
than you'll ever know.

You shall have no other gods before Me.

There is only one God.
Do not worship anyone
or anything else.

You shall not make any false idols or graven images.

Speak politely to
everyone, and do not
use God's name
as a bad word.

You shall not take the name of the Lord your God in vain.

Rest and be thankful for
all that you have.
Enjoy God's blessings at
least one day a week.

Remember the sabbath day, to keep it holy.

Love, honor, and obey your
mother and father.
Be kind to them,
they only want the best for you.

Honor your father and your mother.

Do not hurt others with

your words or actions.

Be friendly and play nice

with everyone.

You shall not murder.

Be faithful and honor your commitments to others.

You shall not commit adultery.

Do not take things that
don't belong to you.
Ask politely
to borrow or share.

You shall not steal.

Be honest and always tell the truth, even when it's hard.

You shall not bear false witness.

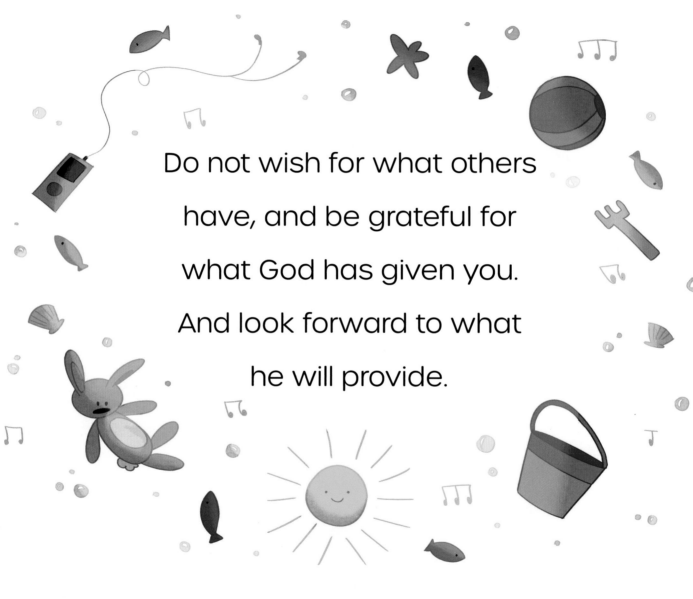

Do not wish for what others have, and be grateful for what God has given you. And look forward to what he will provide.

You shall not covet your neighbor's belongings.

🐾 Claim Your FREE Gift!

Visit ➡️ <u>PDICBooks.com/10gift</u>

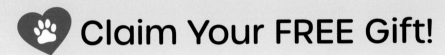

Thank you for purchasing The Ten Commandments, and welcome to the Puppy Dogs & Ice Cream family.

We're certain you're going to love the little gift we've prepared for you at the website above.